Defining Defense:
The 1985 Military Budget

Earl C. Ravenal

Defining
Defense

Defining Defense: The 1985 Military Budget

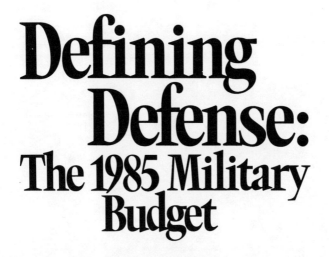

Earl C. Ravenal

CATO INSTITUTE

Library of Congress Cataloging in Publication Data

Ravenal, Earl C.
    Defining defense.

    Includes bibliographical references.
    1. United States—Armed Forces—Appropriations
and expenditures.   2. United States—Military policy.
I. Title.
UA23.R19   1984   355.6'22'0973   84-7001
ISBN 0-932790-40-2

Printed in the United States of America.

CATO INSTITUTE
224 Second Street SE
Washington, D.C. 20003

The Dimensions of the Problem

The salient feature of the first four federal budgets of the Reagan administration has been the vast increase in defense spending. In terms of budget authority—all the funds that are authorized to be spent, though not necessarily in the same year—this administration increased defense spending from 1981 to 1982 by 20 percent, to $211 billion; and from 1982 to 1983 by another 14 percent, to $240 billion. For 1984, Congress granted the administration another 8 percent rise, to $258 billion. And for 1985, the administration is requesting another 18 percent, to $305 billion.

These figures can be put in stark relief against present and projected total budget deficits. The administration's official figures are: for 1982, $110.7 billion; for 1983, $195 billion; for 1984, $184 billion; and for 1985, $180.4 billion. Privately, David Stockman, Director of the Office of Management and Budget, foresees a deficit for 1985 of more than $200 billion, if certain anticipated spending cuts and tax increases are not approved. Some economists have forecast even steeper deficits to follow. For example, Rudolph G. Penner, Director of the Congressional Budget Office, expects federal budget shortfalls rising to $280 billion in 1989; and Michael K. Evans forecasts $330 billion by 1988.[1]

Actually, the precision of these figures—or their stability over weeks and months of forecasting—is not the point. The point is their order of magnitude and the kind of problems they represent. For the predicament in which America finds itself is not a thing of one or two awkward or painful budgetary seasons. It is a dilemma of historic magnitude and import: nothing less than the situation of a mature "imperial" power, beset by multiple political and military challenges in the world but unable to generate sufficient resources for the defense of its extensive global perimeter. The term "imperial" is neutral and generic, not pejorative. Empires, throughout history, have performed certain functions. They fulfill them or they falter and fail. Or their societies and

[1]*The Washington Post*, December 13, 1983; *The Washington Post, Outlook*, December 4, 1983.

leaders may appraise their situations and adjust their foreign policies to fit their capabilities and their true needs and values.

The defense budget must be seen in the context of the larger economic choices. In other words, we must examine what it even means for a nation—not an individual person but a complex social-economic-political system—to "choose" a foreign or military policy. It cannot be an act of pure willfulness. Foreign and, derivatively, military policy are compressed between requirements that arise from our position in the international system (such things as "threats" and "challenges") and the constraints that arise from our domestic system (constraints on resources and support). Requirements can be thought of as demands. Resources and support can be considered as supply factors. It is characteristic of foreign policy bureaucrats, and their chorus among the "foreign policy community," to devote preemptive attention to factors on the demand side, without reference to the other side of the equation. Obviously, a foreign policy that is lopsidedly responsive to threats and challenges, and that *incurs* such pressures through its multiplication of foreign commitments and its assumption of foreign interests, will experience more of the domestic constraints that are latent in any social and economic system.

When we consider these contraints of resources and support, we see that a certain "model" is presented, within which any government must operate. Faced with large deficits, an administration (such as the Reagan administration now) finds its choices limited to five:

1. It could seek to make up the deficits by ordering more taxes. But this would betray crucial promises it made to important constituencies.
2. It could reduce the deficits by making further cuts in domestic programs. But this attempt, commendable to the extent that it has been pursued by the Reagan administration, has run into the area of diminishing budgetary returns for political effort expended.
3. It could try to finance the deficits by borrowing from the banking system—in effect, printing money (as the Federal Reserve System did on a large scale from the late summer of 1982 at least to the spring of 1983). But this behavior, if resumed, would rekindle the fires of inflation.
4. It could borrow in the ordinary credit markets. And so the Reagan administration has done to a large extent.[2] But this has the effect

[2]The dimensions of federal borrowing can be divined from a comparison of federal deficits and other needs with privately generated investable savings—the "total credit pool." For 1985 total federal borrowing, including budgetary needs, off-budget require-

2

of raising interest rates and crowding out industrial recovery and renewal. Up to now, the latter effect has been mitigated by a massive influx of foreign capital, attracted by the high interest rates themselves; but that factor can shift rapidly.

5. Or, of course, the administration could cut its defense program.

These choices can be made, and they can be mixed, but they cannot be evaded or transcended. It is only in terms of these implicit choices that the question—can the country afford its foreign policy?—can be answered.

Let us concentrate on the case for higher taxes. Most arguments for the "affordability" of high defense spending are implicit arguments for more taxation. Couldn't the nation "decide" to assume the burden of substantially increased taxes (and perhaps also that moral equivalent of taxation, conscription)? One article puts the matter thus: "Under John Kennedy in 1961, this country spent 9 percent of its gross national product—half the federal budget—on defense. Today we allocate only a bit more than 6 percent of GNP, a quarter of the federal budget, to defense. . . . What has changed in this country over two decades is the addition of so many other costly activities and income-redistribution programs . . ."[3] This may be historically true, but we are situated in a web of economic and political factors, and our choices are where we find them now, not where they might have been two decades ago. The fact that domestic social welfare expenditures have overtaken—and putatively preempted—defense expenditures does not mitigate the situation; it certainly doesn't make defense more affordable. Quite the contrary, it makes it even less affordable. If anything, it argues for reducing *both* social welfare spending and defense spending. It simply means that our fiscal sins of the past era are finally catching up with us.

But why not, then, more taxes? It is often said that the United States, in the global scheme, is one of the most undertaxed nations. Compar-

---

ments, and the financing of government-sponsored corporations, will be $274.4 billion. This compares with $262.2 billion projected for 1984 and $281 billion in 1983. The 1983 federal borrowing figure represented 56.5 percent of the national pool of credit. This compares with 1974, when a deficit of $4.7 billion and additional borrowing took 12.9 percent of the credit pool, and the 1970s, when federal borrowing averaged 4 percent.

[3]John G. Kester, "War and Money," *The Washingtonian,* January 1983. In this argument, administration and congressional conservatives are joined by liberal critics, whose devotion to taxes, as a sort of infinite resource (as in the parable of the loaves and the fishes) is impressive. The difference seems to be that the conservatives know that defense is expensive, but insist that we must pay the price. The liberals somehow think that, if something is necessary, it doesn't really cost anything.

isons are of this order (in terms of tax revenues as a percentage of gross domestic product): Sweden 51 percent, the Netherlands 46 percent, France 43 percent, Germany 37 percent, the United Kingdom 37 percent, the United States 31 percent, and Japan 27 percent.[4] Thus, some critics attribute our present financial strain to the Reagan administration's initial tax reductions. Its 1981 tax cut ostensibly "measured about $960 billion (in static terms) over the 1982–87 period." But that tax rebate was "69 percent repealed before it was passed, by scheduled Social Security tax increases and bracket creep of $660 billion. . . . The 1982 tax increase repealed a further $229 billion. . . . The recent gasoline tax hike chipped away $16 billion, leaving $55 billion. This small residual would be reduced to zero by a three-year deferral of income tax indexing or transformed into a $35 billion tax increase if scheduled payroll tax increases are moved forward to 1984."[5]

Nevertheless, *The Washington Post* says that "the government needs to raise taxes by more than $100 billion annually to close the budget's built-in deficit in 1988."[6] Leon Wieseltier, in "The Great Nuclear Debate," says, denying entirely the imperative of choice: "If the MX, or any other equally expensive weapon, can be shown to be essential to the country's security, the money should go to it. The government can tax; and only because it has refused to tax does it seem as if we must choose between Social Security and national security."[7] And the "Bipartisan Appeal to the President and Congress on the Budget Situation" (the Peterson Group) would impose $60 billion a year in new taxes, starting in Fiscal Year 1985.

Some economists, not necessarily supply-side Republicans, assert that this country can completely avoid the stringent trade-offs. Charles Schultze, Chairman of the Council of Economic Advisors under President Carter, stated: "The United States is fortunate in having an economy that, with proper policies, can adjust to about as high or as low a level of defense spending as the nation and its leaders think is appropriate. . . . Decisions about the proper long-run level of defense spending should not be determined principally by economic considerations."[8] The critical condition Schultze posits is that "the government must levy

---

[4]Figures are from 1981.

[5]Paul Craig Roberts, "Big Taxes and Big Deficits," *The Wall Street Journal*, January 14, 1983.

[6]Editorial, April 8, 1983.

[7]*The New Republic*, January 10 & 17, 1983.

[8]*The Brookings Bulletin*, Vol 18, No. 2 (Fall 1981).

taxes to soak up the added purchasing power created when goods are produced for it." But this, of course, just points to the further decisions a nation must make if it "chooses" to raise military spending, or even to maintain the existing high level in the face of looming budgetary deficits.

The fact that there are options, such as greatly increased taxes, does not make them more desirable, even if they were politically feasible. There are costs, though in the case of taxation they are diffused (thus its attraction for liberal planners). Higher taxes reduce productivity and incentives while distorting price relationships between competing economic factors. Among other things, taxes reduce the marginal efficiency of the nation's capital by depriving it of part of its returns.

And is there any real difference, after all, between a nation's being "unable" to afford something, such as defense, and its "not wanting" to pay for it? As individuals, we have the advantage of introspection, in order to make such distinctions, and judgments, about our wants and our capabilities. But in the case of systems, it is not possible—indeed, it is not even valid or meaningful—to introspect about their motives and values. And so what a system can do is bounded by what it wants to do, and, more obviously, vice versa.

It is misleading to say that the American people might "decide" to pay for increased defense through increased taxes, as if that were the end of the argument. They are already paying for it—in the transfer of their resources to government, in the erosion of their savings and capital, in the decay of their industrial base, in stubborn unemployment and reduced consumption and the frayed quality of private and public life.

One who once saw this clearly is Caspar W. Weinberger, now Secretary of Defense. In 1972, just named Secretary of Health, Education and Welfare and before that Director of the Office of Management and Budget, he said: "The nation's total resources being limited, it is necessary to consider what is being given up to meet the threat. . . . Our economy and society cannot withstand another inflationary cycle. . . . The fiscal alternatives are either to hold down spending to the level of full-employment revenues or to raise taxes to cover the deficit. It is possible to argue about the merits of each course, but I am convinced that a tax increase is exactly the wrong answer."[9]

Indeed, all but the most confiscatory increases in tax levels or inven-

[9]Caspar W. Weinberger et al., *The Defense Budget* (Washington, D.C.: American Enterprise Institute, 1972).

tions of new imposts would hardly close the budgetary gap. Since our target must be at least $200 billion a year of federal spending cuts, defense must still carry its share—and that share should be more than half of the budgetary gap.

But even if the government could, in theory, balance its books by exacting more resources, in the form of taxes and conscription, to support a large defense establishment and extensive commitments, that would be just the end of one problem and the beginning of another. Solvency, in its largest significance, means that the external and internal stances of this country comport with each other. Resources (and support) are not automatically granted; to be available to the state, they must be mobilized from society, which is the base and context of the state. An extensive, engaged foreign policy and a large, active military posture require big, intrusive, demanding government. If—as we were promised—this is supposed to be a more reserved, less extensive government, then we must have a more detached, disengaged foreign policy. The dilemma is especially cruel for the conservative president who told us, in his inaugural address, that "government is the problem."

The Critics of Defense

There is no lack of critics of defense; but almost all their critiques fall short of sufficiency, and sometimes also miss the necessary conditions, because they mistake the structure and dynamics of defense spending. You can't make an effective prognosis unless you master the diagnosis. If you would save, you have to know where the money is.

This method of analysis seems to elude most "liberal" commentators on defense, who prefer to attribute large and ascending defense expenditures to various devil theories—usually the ministrations of right-wing ideologues, mindless bureaucratic momentum or mindful bureaucratic self-serving, paranoid obsessions with "threats," or the incubus of a "military-industrial complex" whose suboptimizations somehow become preemptive national policy.

Their remedies spring from their analyses. Thus, some would cut support and overhead without cutting combat units, causing unbalanced forces unfit to fight, or fight for long. Some impugn inferior weapons systems, or systems unsuited to the environments in which they would be likely to be used, but usually without proposing substitutes, except a collection of notional characteristics that amount to sheer verbalisms. Some would "stretch out" weapons purchases, not realizing that this drives up unit costs, since the weapons eventually must be bought. Some would simply eliminate a "hit list" of troublesome or notorious weapons, not understanding that something quite similar must be substituted as long as we retain the forces that must be equipped. Some prescribe across-the-board cuts—percentage reductions—without admitting that these might have effects on military readiness, the ability to project force, or the capacity to support alliances. Others urge selective commitment or deployment, without, however, relinquishing the situations that might require the main elements of American forces. Some would change our foreign policy formulas, "stressing" certain areas of the world instead of the present ones—usually, in the contemporary setting, "concentrating" on the Persian Gulf or the sea lanes, but, again, not giving up the other military missions and so actually adding force requirements to those we already have. Such commentators, for the most part diplomatists rather than strategists, think that foreign policy is essentially a cost-free exercise that consists of "signaling" intent, or establishing "presence," or shifting "emphasis" from one region to another, or constructing "doctrines" without creating the forces to deal with the additional contingencies that such doctrines would invite.

From time to time, some of the most fervent and dedicated budget-cutters succumb to despair about "getting a handle" on the defense budget. They are daunted by the prospect of "micro-management"—that is, second-guessing the Pentagon on every detail of specification, procurement, expenditure, and deployment. They seem to lack the ability, the technique, to establish the essential relationships that cause the large segments of defense spending. And so, typically, they retreat into what has become known as "fiscal guidance." With fiscal guidance, in the words of one of the most recent of these conceptual retreats, you "put an arbitrary limit on the amount of available money and its rate of growth, and just tell the practitioners to do the best they can. . . . The best rule for politicians for dealing with Generals [and] Admirals . . . may be this: Put the money on the stump and run."[10] We have heard this resigned refrain before, particularly during the Nixon-Laird regime of defense management from 1969 to 1973. Not so oddly, this approach is seconded by those analysts of governmental policies known as the "bureaucratic politics" school.

The problem with fiscal guidance is threefold: First, any savings that might be achieved by such gross and arbitrary imposition on expenditure, especially in an area so potentially vital and presumably externally determined as national security, will be transient. They are sure to be overtaken by some putative "threat" or some indicated "shortfall" in meeting requirements. Second, the force structures and major weapons systems, and the doctrines and tactics, that result from this process will probably be a gross mismatch of defensive instruments to offensive challenges or alliance requisites. No one will long be satisfied—defense planners, executive branch politicians, or allies. Third, the more far-reaching problems that may exist in the defensive stance of the United States—its deterrent strategy, its alliance commitments—can never be addressed by such a superficial and arbitrary, even cynical, procedure as fiscal guidance.

Thus, neither will the a-rational bureaucratic politics theories invented

[10]Alice M. Rivlin, the outgoing Director of the Congressional Budget Office, in an address to the incipient bureaucrats at the commencement exercises of the Rand Graduate Institute, April 29, 1983.

to explain defense decision-making be a valid guide, nor will the arbitrary measures conceived in ignorance and desperation to cap the rise of defense spending be efficacious. What is needed is analysis that is capable of deriving a true "bottom line"—that is, deriving defense dollars and military manpower from major weapons systems, forces, and doctrines and tactics; then, in turn, from military strategies for various regions and situations; then from "national strategies" or "grand strategies" (that is, large-scale ways of relating to a strategic environment); and finally, from foreign policies.

Two widely credited explanatory fallacies, however, stand in the way and should be dealt with. One of these is nicely captured in the remark of David Stockman, Director of the Office of Management and Budget, that the Pentagon is "a swamp of $10 to $20 to $30 billion worth of waste that can be ferretted out." That is the pseudo-explanation that public seems to appreciate. In another illustrative remark, the editor of *The Washingtonian* poses the question, "Do we get our money's worth [out of the Pentagon]?" and reports: "I asked several Washingtonians—none of them defense experts—and the general feeling was that they didn't know, but doubted it. Their image of the Pentagon was: There is a lot of waste in procurement, with cost overruns, buddy buddy deals, and gold-plating of weapons. The Pentagon will pay $300 for a ladder we'd buy at a hardware store for $39.95. Many weapons are overdesigned and poorly made, and wouldn't work in combat."[11]

In fact, for many months now, we have been treated by the media to a daily soap opera of waste, fraud, and mismanagement in the Pentagon. Journalists have been literally rummaging through military parts bins, and they have finally found a defense issue worthy of their talents. They have come up with $400 claw hammers and monkey wrenches, and—the greatest of horrors so far—a plastic cap for the leg of navigators' stools, from Boeing Inc., that cost the Pentagon $916. Of course, these procurement practices are ridiculous, sad, outrageous. But we have to put them in perspective. The Reagan defense budget request for 1985 is $305 billion. It takes a pile of stool caps, claw hammers, and monkey wrenches to total up to $305 billion, even if they are gold plated or made of titanium.

Moreover, waste, in any strict sense of the word, amounts to only a few billion dollars a year. And despite some commendable efforts in and out of the Pentagon, waste in the procurement and deployment

[11]January 1983.

of forces and weapons is, over time, virtually a constant. First of all, a certain level of incompetence and malfeasance is built into any human activity, even private organizations, let alone public institutions, which produce no real goods, serve no real customers, and strive for no real profits. Second, the waste that exists is not easily recoverable. It is not all in one convenient place, but is distributed almost randomly over a myriad of programs and activities. Therefore, you can't expect to make surgical excisions of fat, sparing the bone and muscle of the programs themselves. Ironically, if you are serious about retaining defense programs, you must plan to fund the waste along with the substance, or you will end up cutting the substance along with the waste.

The second illusion is that of "military reform." Military reform has become a movement that includes among its ardent members a collection of weapons experts, former systems analysts, professors, editorialists of opinion-making journals, disenchanted retired military officers, and aspiring presidential politicians. It is a remarkable coalition of conservatives and liberals, all the way from the Heritage Foundation to *The New Republic*.[12] Essentially, military reform means revising force structures, major weapons systems (and some minor ones, too), troop deployments, and fighting doctrines. It also emphasizes military education, "strategy" instead of "management," and inculcating troop "leadership." It aims to conserve resources, yet enjoy the same or even greater combat output or deterrent effect. There is the familiar suggestion that our forces could be made "leaner and tougher"—indeed that leaner *is* tougher.

One editorialist has summarized the thrust of that movement: "A sensible defense policy—one that builds weapons that are workable, reliable, and (relatively) cheap instead of overcomplicated, breakable, and wildly expensive . . . and that concentrates on training, maintenance, and readiness rather than on mindless procurement—would yield dramatically more military effectiveness for the same pile of dollars."[13] And so it would—if it could. But wishing for such weapons is

---

[12]Examples of this genre of criticism are: Barry R. Posen and Stephen W. Van Evera, "Overarming and Underwhelming," *Foreign Policy*, Fall 1980; Jeffrey G. Barlow, ed., *Reforming the Military* (Washington, D.C.: The Heritage Foundation, 1981); James Fallows, *National Defense* (New York: Random House, 1981); and George W. S. Kuhn, "Defense," in Richard N. Holwill, ed., *Agenda '83* (Washington, D.C.: The Heritage Foundation, 1983). *Time* devoted a major article and a front cover to the military reform movement (March 7, 1983), including the guerrilla campaign for honest costing and procurement waged within the Pentagon by systems analyst Franklin C. Spinney.

[13]*The New Republic*, October 14, 1981.

not creating them. For the real defect in these proposals is not what they promise, but what they can't deliver. A few military horror stories don't add up to a conclusive critique, and a handful of therapeutic adjectives is not an effective remedy. Those cheap, sensible weapons must get at their targets, and maybe get back, in intensive battlefield environments. It isn't dim-witted generals and grasping defense contractors (the stuff of current mythology) that are driving up the price of our forces and weapons. It is determined, capable adversaries and the requisites of modern combat. Our choice, therefore, is not whether to have those expensive forces and weapons or not. It is whether to fight in those environments and against those adversaries, or not.

Among other things, the military reformers are not properly conservative. They would substitute "maneuver" for firepower, and make our defense dependent on a critical supply of brilliant tacticians and inspiring combat leaders. They tend to confuse brilliance and inspiration with the more complex and mundane problems of fielding a global military force of several million men and tens of thousands of weapons systems, and trying to confer on that force sustainable advantages on the intensive battlefields of the future.

In other words, we are talking, not about defense as such, but about buying confidence in defense. There is a difference between what you try to do with the forces and weapons you already have and what you must prudently *plan* on accomplishing, in large-scale, complex defense efforts, long before the fact of battle or the outbreak of war.

Besides, leaner is not always tougher; it may just be skinnier. And smarter is not always cheaper. Indeed, military reformers, for the most part, would not even translate "smarter" into "cheaper." They would cash the reforms in for more weapons, more forces, more overseas presence, more alliance commitment. Their schemes may be "cost-effective." But cost-effectiveness—and this has always been its problem, since its introduction in the regime of Secretary of Defense Robert S. McNamara—does not tell you where you are on the famous all-purpose curve of diminishing returns; whether you are on the satisfying "steep" or the disappointing "flat." Above all, it doesn't tell you whether you can afford the next increment of cost; or, for that matter, whether you need the next increment of effectiveness—whether it represents indispensable national security or something less, such as the protection of other countries.

The assertions of the military reformers are not even immune from detailed technical criticism and rebuttal. For example, the so-called "Gary Hart" pocket aircraft carriers (800 feet, 40,000 tons, oil-fired), might cost three-quarters as much as the present Nimitz-class carriers (1,000 feet, 91,400 tons, nuclear-powered). And so two of those smaller ones "could carry 76 aircraft vs. 98 for one *Nimitz*, and. . . . the cost per aircraft base would be $245-million for the small carrier vs. $121-million for the large carrier."[14] You can't replace something with nothing, or with something merely notional. It has to be hardware, and when they are required to specify their alternative hardware, the reformers invite the same criticism that they level against present defense programs and weapons systems.

Then again, with military reform, there is the problem of sufficiency. In other words, these critiques beg a further question: Even if we were to adopt the proposed reforms, would they save enough to allow the United States to renew its lease on the world? So military reform ultimately distracts us from considering the feasibility of our global mission. In their obsession with the details, the military reformers overlook the more comprehensive logic of the defense problem this country faces. Defense, if we want it or if we must have it, is expensive. It may be that the objects of our foreign policy, because of the means that must be used to protect them, are priced out of our reach.

The greatest military horror stories lie not in malfeasance of procurement, malfunctioning weapons systems, or technical idiocy, but rather in the weapons that *do* work. We shall consider one of the principal building blocks of our defense effort, the cornerstone of the Navy— the aircraft carrier. Before we begin, it is well to point out that the problem does not lie in the choice between a Nimitz-class carrier or some notional "Gary Hart" carrier—which one might be more efficient or more cost-effective. The gross cost of the entire carrier battle group, whether it had a maxi or a mini carrier as its centerpiece, would be roughly the same, if we were to include, as we should, its share of Navy administrative and training costs, its share of Pentagon overhead, and what it takes in our force structure to put one of these task forces forward, where it counts. Nor does the problem lie in the faulty design of this ship, or its complement of aircraft, or its fleet of escort vessels and replenishment ships. The problem is more basic and intractable— the economics of modern warfare. And of this problem the aircraft carrier is a parable.

Here are the statistics. The next aircraft carrier we buy, a Nimitz-

---

[14]*Armed Forces Journal International,* September 1982, p. 44. And these figures obviously do not even include the 2:1 rearward-forward ratio; the 2:1 30-year operating-procurement cost ratio; and the 2:1 overhead-direct cost ratio. See the analysis below.

class nuclear carrier, will cost about $3.8 billion. Another $3 billion will be spent for its complement of 98 aircraft of various types (most of them to defend the carrier itself); a further $4 billion for about 6 escort ships, including the controversial AEGIS-class anti-aircraft cruiser, which itself costs over a billion dollars, and a screen of attack submarines; another $2 billion for a miscellany of replenishment vessels and support systems; and perhaps $2 billion more for this battle group's share of the building and acquisition of shore facilities. So far, we have arrived at a total of some $14.8 billion, just to *acquire* this hardware and fixed support. If we add $29.6 billion to man and operate these ships and facilities over their 30-year life (a kind of rule of thumb), we are up to about $44.4 billion. And that is not all. For each carrier task force on line, we have to allow for two more in the rear—one in reserve and one in overhaul. And so we arrive at this calculation: The 30-year total to sustain one carrier forward is $133 billion.

But those numbers are only for the carrier groups and their *specific* support; we are not yet including their share of general costs of the United States Navy (some Navy intelligence and communications, reserve forces, logistical functions, some training, medical, and other personnel activities, and some miscellaneous administrative and associated activities) and, above that, their share of the cost of the Defense Department (overall intelligence and communications, research and development, overall logistics, general personnel activities, and defense-wide administration). If we were to do that—and here, admittedly, we are in the area of gross and even conjectural calculations—we would have to triple the cost again (since producing and projecting forces amount to perhaps only three-eighths of the whole cost of a military service, and, on top of that, general overhead adds perhaps another 12 percent), and we would arrive at a comprehensive total of some $400 billion, over the lifetime of one forward carrier deck (and this in only 1985 dollars). (That calculation is roughly corroborated in a different calculation below, that deals with the costs of major components of our forces. When we talk about the portion of Navy surface forces that is devoted to our 13 carrier battle groups, we find that, for 1985, it costs $13.27 billion a year in total comprehensive costs, already including all Navy and Defense overheads, to put one of those carrier battle groups forward. If we multiply the annual figure by 30 years to arrive at the lifetime cost, we also get approximately $400 billion.)

That is the "input" side of the equation. Now, what about the "output" side? What is the payoff for this investment? That $400 billion buys the ability to project at sea or onto some distant shore about 35 attack sorties a day—that is, 35 individual flights of a single aircraft, each carrying perhaps six to eight tons of bombs. And that presumes each flight reaches its target, hits it, and returns safely to its ship (otherwise, of course, the output will be even less). In other words, for $400 billion we increase our greatness as a nation by the capability to wage 35 attack sorties a day (or, to be fair, to patrol a few of the world's sea lanes).

The purpose of all this is not to tell military horror stories, but to illustrate how the economics of defense and the realities of foreign policy come together on the fulcrum of the major units of the force structure. It might seem that the aircraft carrier exemplifies the "big-ticket item" that is so much the target of contemporary defense criticism. But it is not the procurement costs of this weapons system, egregious as they are, that are at issue here—as if the system could simply be dispensed with. Rather, it is the cost of this system as an element in the *force structure* that matters in the end.

Forces and Missions

There is only one way to cut defense costs—that is, for more than one or two seasons, or without hopelessly unbalancing the very forces that are counted on to perform whatever residual missions they are assigned—and that is by cutting *force structure*. That, in turn, means eliminating the missions of these deleted forces; and that implies substantive changes in our foreign policies. I do not necessarily mean formal changes, but rather the changes that are implicit in our international relationships because those rest on our capabilities. (We must define "foreign policy," not as a bunch of verbal predilections, but as the sum of the contingent responses we would make in the hypothetical circumstances in which those moves would be called for. The sum of these "if-then" propositions constitutes our foreign policy.)

The disability—indeed, the pathology—of all the other critiques, and what renders them so transient, so easily overturned by pressing circumstances or even by sustained, probing debate, is that they would retain the same foreign policies but would trim the means to carry them out. The other critiques attempt, at some point, to abrogate the logic of defense, in order to be free of its demanding requisites. In some ways, such evasive critiques are more dangerous than the more straightforward proposals and requisitions of the present administration.

If savings are desired, I suggest that would-be military reformers begin by determining "where the money is"—that is, what strategic tasks, missions, and functions are responsible for the major categories and amounts of defense spending. Consequently I offer an anatomy and a *methodology* that might serve to relate the exactions and expenditures of resources to national strategies and ultimately to foreign policies. Such a methodology enables a fairly confident and revealing attribution of defense expenditures to the major components of the military services and, more important, to the regions we are committed to defend. Only by performing this exercise, which is essentially *rational* and presumes a process of reasoning—though not necessarily the substantive correctness or unique validity of any particular premises—can we identify those policies that require the defense dispositions and

15

material resources that we devote to them, and thus, to the extent that we hope for some alternative policy, can we know *what to change* in order to secure that alternative.

Where is the real money to be found in the defense budget? It is in the large aggregate combat forces, and in turn the broad missions of those forces in the world. To understand this, an anatomy lesson is in order. The dollar figures in the following examples are slices of the Reagan administration's requested 1985 defense budget authorization (not the "outlay," which trails the authorization in a period of rising expenditures). That requested authorization is $305 billion.

Strategic nuclear forces (including, as they should, their full share of military support costs and Pentagon overheads) come to about $70 billion, or 23 percent of the 1985 requested authorization.

All the rest, $235 billion or 77 percent, is dedicated to general purpose forces—land divisions, tactical air wings, and surface naval units. Some specific costs of major components of our general purpose forces are as follows: An average Army division will cost over $4.8 billion, and we will have 17 of them. A wing of tactical aircraft will cost about $2.1 billion, and we will have the equivalent of 44 of these. The Marine Corps will cost $21 billion. The full cost of deploying one aircraft carrier battle group forward, in the West Pacific or the Indian Ocean or the North Atlantic or the Mediterranean, will be over $13 billion, and our strategy requires us to keep four or five forward.

But to put the defense budget in the sharpest perspective, we need to move beyond the cost of elements of the force structure to a geographical cross-section. Pentagon budgeteers would complain that attributing particular units to particular regional missions distorts the picture. They claim that many units have double assignments—for example, that a brigade of the First Cavalry Division, based in the American Southwest, is targeted for Europe as well as the Persian Gulf as part of the Rapid Deployment Forces. But that is double-counting, and in view of Secretary of Defense Weinberger's insistence on "defending all theaters simultaneously," it violates the First Law of Thermodynamics, too. Moreover, the two areas are very different, and a unit such as the First Cavalry has to train, equip, and configure itself for one or the other primary responsibility.

In any event, by my own estimates (derived from an analysis of Secretary Weinberger's 1985 "Posture Statement," presented to Congress on February 1, 1984), Europe will continue to be the main beneficiary of American defense resources in 1985, accounting for $129 billion. Asia will absorb $47 billion. And an expanding requirement for

Rapid Deployment Forces will take $59 billion, of which about $47 billion is for the Persian Gulf. (In 1985, the Pentagon will continue to increase its primary allocation of forces to the Persian Gulf. It will begin to implement a plan to create as many as five additional "light" Army divisions, justified mostly by the Persian Gulf or Southwest Asia requirement, but without adding any significant manpower to the Army.)

A Note on Methodology

Where do these figures come from? It may be useful to give a more detailed account of the methodology by which I arrive at these numbers. This methodology is not obscure or tricky, once we understand some ground rules.

There are two sets of calculations. In one calculation, the rough number of basic combat units (divisions, wing equivalents, important ships) in each of the four military services (Army, Navy, Air Force, and Marine Corps, splitting off the Marine Corps from the Navy in a manner that captures the Navy overhead devoted to supporting the Marines) is divided into the entire manpower of that service and the entire budget of that service (the latter having been adjusted to absorb its share of defense agencies, defense-wide activities, civil defense, and military assistance). This first calculation tells us the full annual cost of procuring and keeping each basic combat unit. It is also useful for construing the manpower and budget implications of alternative force structures.

In this calculation we count only *combat* forces as defense outputs. Everything else in the defense budget—such as defense agencies, defense-wide activities, civil defense, and military assistance—must be considered as a support cost or overhead. A related point is that we calculate "full slices," including the support and overhead, as the real cost of those combat forces.

Pentagon budgeteers will complain that it makes no sense to allocate certain categories of support and overhead, such as, in the extreme case, retirement pay, to combat functions. And in a strict sense, this is a valid complaint. But, although full-slice costing may sometimes seem arbitrary, in an important sense it is more accurate than the traditional costing of the military services, which represents costs, and thus potential savings from reductions, as merely marginal. As the Pentagon "Whiz Kids" in the department of Systems Analysis used to say: "It's better to be roughly right than precisely wrong." If we don't include all support and overhead, we will be seriously *under*costing what it takes, in the longer run, to produce forces. Moreover, the Pentagon's favored marginal numbers, used to depict the "costs" of all forces, do not add up to the total defense budget. Something is missing (calling

18

to mind Ronald Reagan's classic line, "Where's the rest of me?"). Or, to put it another way, if you fail to allocate all costs, in theory you could eliminate all the "cutting edge," all the combat outputs, and still have half of the defense budget left. Of course, support costs and overhead do not diminish automatically with cuts in the more conspicuous combat forces. Like any fixed costs in industry, they must be decreased by decision. That is, it takes the guts to cut them as well as the intelligence to identify them. Finally, if you were selling defense as a product—which, in a sense, the government is doing, to the taxpayers—if you failed to include and recover all indirect costs, you would eventually go broke.

In the second calculation, we attribute all forces either to the "strategic" or to the "general purpose" side of the ledger, and, in turn, attribute general purpose forces to some region of the world. Again, for this calculation, combat forces are costed on a full-slice basis. For failing to state the full cost of forces prevents us from linking defense dollars and manpower with the defense of regions of the world. It makes the linkage unintelligible. Both full-slice costing and the allocation of forces to regions of the world are necessary to making defense costs *intelligible*—that is, relating the primary inputs to the ultimate outputs. Perhaps that is why defense officials are so apparently intent on diffusing or obscuring these connections. In the last analysis, it is a matter of "truth in packaging" or "truth in labeling"—telling taxpayers where their money is going. Of course, the Pentagon and other national security agencies don't always fail to identify the full costs of an activity. It depends on the season of the budget year. When attempting to justify its entire defense budget request, or when demonstrating to our allies that we are paying a disproportionate share of the costs of an alliance, the Pentagon prefers to state its costs fully. But when defending against proposed cuts, it claims that deleting this or that unit or program from the force structure or the budget would save only the tip of its marginal costs.

One way of "trapping" the costs of defending regions of the world has been to take the *Defense Posture Statement* and refer to a table in the appendix of that book which sets forth the 10 defense "programs," or apparent defense output categories.[15] Only the first two programs, however, Strategic (nuclear) Forces and General Purpose (conventional

---

[15]That particular table does not appear in the 1985 posture statement. Therefore, we must restore it by extrapolating the figures for all 10 program categories from the 1984 figures.

and tactical nuclear) Forces, are true combat functions or true output categories; thus we must distribute the other eight categories over the first two, in appropriate measure. Then to get the costs of defending each region of the world, we must multiply the cost of general purpose forces by a fraction representing the active land divisions (both Army and Marine) attributable to this region—not just the divisions deployed there, but those procured and maintained primarily for contingencies in the region—over the entire number of active land divisions. (Land divisions are the most practical and the most accessible measure, and they quite well represent the allocation of tactical air wings, whether Air Force, Navy, or Marine.) The Pentagon traditionally divides the world into only three regions: (1) NATO/Europe and its southern flank, which is the Eastern Mediterranean; (2) Asia, meaning East Asia and the Western Pacific; and (3) "Other Regions and the Strategic Reserve," which includes what is now called the Rapid Deployment Forces or the "Central Command," which in turn includes Southwest Asia, comprising mostly the Persian Gulf area. The geographical attributions of forces must be checked against all rationales and descriptions in the report of the Secretary of Defense and other sources.

Of course, there is no law that prevents forces kept for one regional contingency from being used for another. The last articulate and sophisticated discussion of the regional rationale for general purpose forces was conducted by Secretary of Defense James R. Schlesinger.[16] Schlesinger referred to "a planning algorithm" for regional force allocation, and was quite specific about the degree of arbitrariness, as well as the degree of "reality," in this calculation. Schlesinger's analysis, however, was intended mostly to demonstrate that the force structure designed for the "major challenges," the "very demanding contingencies," is also adequate for lesser "off-design" cases, such as our resupply operation in the October 1973 Middle East war. He was not trying to prove that there is *no* relationship between the theater contingencies and the forces. Despite the intellectual disruption of the Nixon administration's shift from the previous doctrine of "2½ wars" to "1½ wars," and its notion of swing forces that might serve in several different geographical theaters, no one has yet abrogated the connection between contingencies and forces. Therefore, the critical policy variable remains the projected American response to the contingency: If we ceased to plan for the most demanding specific contingencies, the force structure could

[16]*Annual Defense Department Report, FY 1975* (Washington, D.C.: U.S. Government Printing Office, March 4, 1974), pp. 84–85.

be considerably reduced. In fact, if we took Schlesinger at face value—not treating the large wars as simultaneous and therefore not treating their requirements as additive—we should want to know why the force structure he requested was not much lower. And, though Schlesinger was correct in his implication that *cutting* a contingency, such as Asia, would not produce a *pari passu* cut of the forces necessary for that region, nevertheless his proposition does not apply symmetrically: If one builds forces from the ground up, contingency by contingency, one can arrive at a certain explicit structure.

I judge that, for FY 1985, the Reagan administration intends the following regional attribution of a total of 20 active ground divisions: NATO/Europe, 11 divisions; East Asia, 4 divisions; Other Regions and the Strategic Reserve, 5 divisions. These allocations are likely to continue to change as proportionately more forces are "pointed" primarily at Southwest Asia, at the expense mostly of Europe and (to some extent) of East Asia. Applying these fractions to the total cost of our general purpose forces, $235 billion, we can calculate the rough cost of our three regional commitments.

National Strategy

What this anatomy lesson ought to demonstrate is that defense budgets are not for nothing; they are *for something.* The dollars buy forces, the forces have missions; the missions are in regions where the United States has defensive commitments or supposed strategic interests; the strategic involvements, in sum, are practically equivalent to the nation's foreign policy. Therefore, defense budgets cannot be cut significantly— on a scale, say, commensurate with our federal deficit problem—without consequences for their objects: our alliances, our foreign policies. Those who would cut must decide—tell us, and admit to themselves— what they would do without.

None of the cuts suggested by the defense critics touches the longer-term and larger question of the solvency of our national strategy and, beyond that, of our foreign policy. Eight years ago,[17] I said that defense was expensive—more expensive than liberals, in particular, were willing to believe—and that, in the longer run, the implementation of our foreign policy was outrunning our material and social resources. Those propositions still hold. The question now is whether the United States will have to go beyond minor and superficial adjustments and confront the entire "paradigm" of its national strategy—the way we have done our strategic business in the world since the early Cold War.

Several decades ago, Walter Lippmann, in a classic critique, said: "In foreign relations, as in all other relations, a policy has been formed only when commitments and power have been brought into balance."[18] Lippmannesque critiques are experiencing something of a revival, though still a modest one.[19] But arguments from solvency function better in

---

[17]"After Schlesinger: Something Has to Give," *Foreign Policy*, Spring 1976.

[18]*U.S. Foreign Policy: Shield of the Republic* (Boston: Atlantic-Little Brown, 1943). The first Secretary of Defense, James Forrestal, began his first report to Congress in 1948: "It is our duty to see that our military potential conforms to the requirements of our national policy; in other words, that our policy does not outstrip our power."

[19]Critics who have written in this vein lately are James Chace, *Solvency: The Price of Survival* (New York: Random House, 1981); and David Calleo, "Inflation and American Power," *Foreign Affairs*, Spring 1981, and *The Imperious Economy* (Cambridge, Mass.: Harvard University Press, 1982).

the critical than the creative mode. They tend to pose the choices, not make the choice. Often they end merely in a reiteration of the alternatives. For instance, do we reduce our forces in Europe, after all, or do we resign ourselves to bearing the domestic inflationary costs of supporting those forces? In the final analysis, which term would these critics insist on as fixed and which would they allow to float? Faced with that stern requirement, even the solvency critics sometimes suggest that we can find some way to avoid the choice. Here, for instance, is James Chace in the peroration of his book: "Since foreign policy commitments can finally only be validated by war, the essential condition for our defense is to maintain military forces capable of fulfilling these commitments. . . . In foreign relations as in domestic affairs, the way to restore the balance between our commitments and our power is to increase our means and, in this way, to regain our lost solvency." This is to restate the problem at the end, more or less as the author found it at the beginning.

Even Lippmann failed to distinguish between policies based simply on inadequate means and policies based on means that are impossible or improbable for a society to generate. The question of solvency has now entered a post-Lippmann phase. It is not enough just to invoke the potential power to balance our commitments. To test the validity of those commitments, it is now necessary to assess the underpinnings of that power, which are mostly domestic. There are several paths to solvency. One is to prescribe the means, somehow, to support a demanding foreign policy. The other is to stop living, strategically and geopolitically, beyond our means.

If substantial cuts had to be made in the defense budget, how would we handle such an injunction? That invokes the model of strategic choice. Since the United States assumed the obligations of alliance, we have faced a tight array of options:

- We could assume the burdens of high-confidence conventional defense, with the necessity of preparing large and timely reinforcements.
- Or we could accept the risks of substantial reliance on nuclear defense, including the option of first use; that is, we could lower the nuclear threshold, or just keep it at an already low level.
- Or we could admit the prospect of conventional defeat in the theater, without escalating or reinforcing.
- There is, of course, another alternative: We could lower the required level of defensive effort. This could be done either by arms control that would truly bind the adversary and thus reduce the threat—

if this is attainable—or by disengagement from our commitments to defend other countries. We could disengage partially, by devolving some defensive responsibilities to allies or proxies, possibly with a compensatory transfer of arms (what was, in its time, called the Nixon Doctrine); or we could disengage entirely, by sloughing off military alliances.

That is the box. There are no other ways to go. Some might ask: Well, couldn't we just muddle through (as if muddling could achieve evasion or transcendence of the alternatives)? Not really. The "choices" a complex society or political system makes are not always explicitly declared, but they are made nonetheless. To the extent that an administration, even one that disguises the logic of its actions with the most artful diplomatic communication, fails to assume the risks of nuclear deterrence or the burdens of high-confidence conventional defense or fails to negotiate them reliably away, it implicitly accepts defeat, or even disengagement of the United States from the fate of its allies.

The point is that the choices cannot be rigged to suit preference or predilection. They are substantive and they involve hard trade-offs; you have to give up something to get something else. If you do not wish to defend in certain ways, and can't defend in others, then you have to give up certain missions in the world, which means that you have to give up parts of the world, contingently. President Reagan got the sense of this when he asked of those who would cut the defense budget: "Which interests and which commitments are they prepared to abandon?"[20]

Significant cuts would affect our entire stance of containment of the Soviet Union and Soviet-inspired communism, the stance we have maintained over the four decades since the beginning of the cold war in the late 1940s. In that time, the national strategy of the United States has consisted of two basic elements—deterrence, and forward defense or alliance—both devoted to containing communist power and influence. Deterrence is roughly equated with our strategic nuclear forces; we seek to maintain a balance—or better—of strategic nuclear arms with Russia and to provide a nuclear umbrella over our allies and various other countries. Forward defense or alliance involves our protection, mostly by means of general purpose forces, of allies and other countries that occupy strategic positions or have sympathetic social and political values.

Since we are suggesting a change in "national strategy" and "foreign

[20]Radio speech, reported in *The Washington Post*, February 21, 1983.

24

policy," we should define what kinds of things comprise these levels of policy, preparation, and action. National strategy can be seen as the "national security" component or aspect of foreign policy; or it can be seen as a level that mediates between foreign policy in its larger sense and specific military strategies for regions or situations. National strategy relates to such questions as the following:

What kinds of threats should we consider seriously?

How many wars do we plan to fight simultaneously?

What is to be our nuclear threshold?

Which regions of the world is it important to defend militarily?

In general, what should be our attitude toward intervention in conflict in other regions?

How much emphasis are we to place on making nuclear threats as opposed to waging conventional defense?

Or, in general, to what extent should we rely on exemplary, retaliatory exercises of force for deterrence, including, perhaps, terror?

Should we adopt a forward defense or one that depends on a strategic reserve?

Should we favor initial defense, or counterattack to regain lost territory and other strategic objectives?

Should we depend on standing forces or on reserves and mobilization?

Can we use economic sanctions as leverage?

How much should we rely on allies, or proxy forces or nations, rather than unilateral, independent military forces?

Should we place emphasis on supplying, to allies or proxy nations, naval support, air support, nuclear backup, and military assistance?

To what extent should we plan on dispatching or deploying our own ground forces?

How early in conflict situations should we intervene?

What should be our attitude toward initiating preemptive attacks or preventive wars?

How much should we rely on, and respect, the results of mediation and conciliation?

To what extent should we contribute to, participate in, or rely on, multilateral peace-keeping procedures and exercises?

In general, how much insinuation of force should we put behind our diplomacy?

What portion of our national wealth should we devote to our
military defense?

In contrast, foreign policy questions, for a nation in general, but particularly for ours, comprise more the following:

With whom should we be allied?

Should we rely on alliances as an overall orientation for our country
in the world, or should we pursue a more independent foreign
policy, even one of unilateralism?

Should we place relatively more emphasis on military means or on
trade and cultural contacts, in order to achieve influence on the
conduct of other nations?

Do we have any expansionist or irredentist objectives? Are we
trying to gain "natural" borders, or to implement any concept
of national identity, or to include certain ethnic groups within
our area or sphere of interest?

Do we aspire to political or cultural leadership of wider groupings
of people in the world?

Do we aim at leadership of a coalition of nations?

Should we pursue, in general, a "balance of power" policy? Should
we attempt to construct a countervailing coalition to restrain the
ambitions or power projections of other states?

Should we support supranational organizations, such as the United
Nations?

In general, what kind of international order should we favor—
e.g., collective security, a bipolar system of blocs, a multipolar
balance of power, general unalignment?

Should we attempt to detach certain countries (e.g., those of Eastern Europe) from another country's sphere of domination?

How aggressively should we assert our rights of neutrality in
dealing with belligerents?

To what extent should we attempt to pursue "values" in our
international relations?

In particular, should we intervene in other countries' affairs to
preserve or further "human rights"?

In our policy of recognition, should we deal with governments
that simply control certain territory and population, or should
we adopt more idealistic criteria?

To what extent should our national government support the commercial efforts of our own citizens, and private groups such as
multinational corporations that are based on our territory, in

their dealings with other countries or in their competition with groups from other nations?

Should we join other nations in attempts to restrain private commercial activities, by such means as multilateral "codes"?

Should we preserve the oceans as an area free for private or national commerce, exploration, development, and military use? Or should there be international regimes of regulation or exploitation in various functions?

Should we give economic aid to other countries and peoples?

Should such aid be tied to certain reciprocal moves those entities might make that conduce to our own advantage?

Should we promote capitalist or free market systems of economic organization in other countries? Should we make other countries' economic or social systems a criterion for our other dealings with those countries?

What the Reagan Administration is Doing and Not Doing

The problem of solvency presents itself with peculiar poignancy to the Reagan administration as it approaches the end of its first term. After all, these are the people who were going to square the triangle of objectives: large increases in defense spending, fiscal responsibility in the form of eventually balanced budgets, and tax relief as the agent and symbol of releasing the productive powers of the economy. The pity is that the last two could have been attained, but for the first.

But the Reagan administration did not entirely invent its problems. Actually, this administration is trying to implement the defense objectives it inherited. As Secretary of Defense Weinberger put it in his maiden presentation to Congress in 1981, the Carter administration grossly underestimated the demands that Soviet challenges were making on the tangible military responses of the United States; above all, it systematically under-funded its own defense programs, leaving a cumulative shortfall of several hundred billion dollars for its successor to make up. Taken as a relative or conditional judgment, there is a certain wry justice in Weinberger's statement. If you ignore the rhetoric, overlook some of the nuances, and leave out of the calculation those policy objectives that have little consequences for military forces or defense costs, you could judge that what is wrong with Reagan's foreign and military policies is not that they are much different from Carter's, but that they are so much the same. The Reagan administration is just the latest in a long line, Democratic and Republican, from the beginning of the Cold War, to promote the American paradigm of large-scale deterrence and extensive forward defense or alliance. All it has tried to do is spend enough to implement it.

Critics of the Reagan administration have been leveling two kinds of attacks, which are oddly contradictory. The first is that the Reagan administration has vastly expanded America's international goals, and added some novel strategic elements, such as "horizontal escalation" including assaults on Soviet naval forces in their ports, and nuclear "war-winning" through developing the capacity to wage "protracted nuclear war." On the other hand, the critics charge that the Reagan administration has no strategy at all, indeed that it doesn't even have a foreign policy—that it is just throwing money in the general direction of "national security."

That is certainly a case of critical overkill. Both of the critiques can't be true. In a sense, neither of them is. First of all, questions of foreign policy and national strategy are always "answered," more or less explicitly, in the actions, orientations, and dispositions of nations. And national strategies are derived from—and are, in the longer run, consistent with—foreign policies. A nation *has* both, whether or not a presidential speech has enunciated them or a blue-ribbon commission has defined them.

Second, what we find is that the Reagan administration has much the same foreign and military policies as the Carter administration, both in size and substance. For all its increased defense budgetary requests, the Reagan administration has added hardly any manpower or force structure. At most, it has fleshed out some skeleton air wings and upgraded one carrier battle group from a sort of cadre status to a more fully active one; and in 1985 it will begin to develop existing Army units into a few more, lighter, divisions. In the words of William W. Kaufmann: "During fiscal 1981 and 1982 the Reagan administration increased by nearly $7 billion over the Carter estimates those appropriation accounts that fund the operations and support the armed forces. The purpose of this increase was to improve the readiness of existing capabilities. But the administration also increased by more than $25 billion the key investment accounts—procurement and research, development, testing, and evaluation—to accelerate the modernization of the existing force structure and also to take advantage of the economies to be achieved from buying new equipment in large orders."[21] Remarking the continuity of policy and programs, Kaufmann went on to say that the "$32.5 billion [of Reagan requests] more than Carter had proposed in fiscal 1981 and 1982. . . . was to be used to speed completion of the Carter programs and items lower on the armed forces' list of priorities. Virtually no change was proposed in the size of the nuclear and nonnuclear forces or in the way these forces might be used."

As early as November 1981, *Armed Forces Journal International* could conclude that "Ronald Reagan's program to rearm America now adds up to less than a one percent increase in actual defense spending over

[21]"The Defense Budget," in Joseph A. Pechman, ed., *Setting National Priorities: The 1983 Budget* (Washington, D.C.: Brookings Institution, 1982).

29

the Pentagon budgets proposed by former President Jimmy Carter last January for the next three years."[22] What is striking is that, far from being able to fulfill its alleged wish-list of expansive military programs, the Reagan administration has had trouble maintaining a defense budget that is just about at the level that Jimmy Carter might have attained.

If we are willing to screen out much "noise" at intermediate levels of government, we find that the Reagan administration has implemented the programs and strategies of the Carter administration (at least after Afghanistan, in what could be called the "second Carter administration"). In every consequential aspect, the Reagan administration has displayed remarkable continuity: in the strategic dimension, counterforce, war-fighting, and the MX missile; in the general purpose force dimension, the reinstitution of global defense and direct American involvement in regions, featuring the Rapid Deployment Forces and the acquisition of stepping-stone bases; in the Middle East, the policy of active intrusion; with regard to China, the reinforcement of relations; and in the area of arms control, after a late start, a negotiating posture of "deep cuts." Only in Central America has the Reagan administration seemed to go considerably beyond the Carter limits; but by January 1981, Carter's policy had not yet been tested by an evolving Marxist regime in Nicaragua and a polarized political and military situation in El Salvador.

Some of the foreign policy directions that the critics complain about in statements of Secretary of Defense Weinberger are simply restatements or paraphrases of traditional defense department rhetoric—almost on the level of boilerplate, expressing traditional American defense goals. For example, the Secretary's 1984 posture statement poses the following objectives for foreign policy:

> "To preserve our freedom, our political identity, and the institutions that are their foundation—the Constitution and the rule of law.
> "To protect the territory of the United States, its citizens, and its vital interests abroad from armed attack.
> "To foster an international order supportive of the interests of the United States through alliances and cooperative relationships with friendly nations; and by encouraging democratic institutions, economic development, and self-determination throughout the world.
> "To protect access to foreign markets and overseas resources in order to maintain the strength of the United States' industrial, agricultural, and technological base and the nation's economic well-being."

[22]In fact, in terms of outlays, the military budget for 1983 that Jimmy Carter projected in his last month in office, January 1981, was $205.3 billion; Ronald Reagan's actual outlays for 1983 were $205.0 billion.

The first two objectives—with the possible exception of "vital interests abroad"—are so unexceptionable that even a confirmed noninterventionist wouldn't raise an eyebrow. The last two, though far more extensive, are familiar, even tedious, though some critics profess to see in them dangerous departures from the putatively more restricted objectives of previous administrations.

The charge that the Reagan administration has changed American strategy deserves a more extended examination in one crucial area: the ostensible move to a lower nuclear threshold. In what sense might there be grounds for such a charge? Perhaps it is based on the "bellicosity" of this administration's rhetoric, from its campaign in the fall of 1980 to the speeches of the President in the late spring of 1982 in London, Bonn, Berlin, and the United Nations, and for a year thereafter. In a more substantial reproach, much has been made by critics of the Reagan administration's supposed shift to war-fighting, war-winning nuclear strategies.

But I find nothing particularly novel in the utterances of various figures in the Reagan administration to the effect that the United States must design its forces and doctrines so as to "prevail" in a nuclear war. There is nothing even alarming about those statements, beyond what is irreducibly alarming about nuclear confrontation and mutual deterrence themselves. In fact, most of the critics, give or take some verbiage, would come down on virtually the same nuclear strategies as the administration—particularly those critics (and most are in that category) who subscribe to the threat or actual use of America's nuclear weapons to deter or answer an attack on our European allies.

Better to keep one's eyes on the strategy itself, as expressed tangibly in our nuclear posture and our doctrines of targeting and precedence of use. Those are the elements that constitute our nuclear strategy, and the ones that might make a difference in our propensity to go to war, or to escalate to nuclear war. I would argue that, when we examine our nuclear strategy in this light, we will find that the Reagan administration is simply affirming the requisites of our traditional strategy of "extended deterrence"—that is, the use of our nuclear weapons to deter all kinds of threats, conventional or nuclear, to our allies as well as ourselves, and to strategic objects and positions of less than truly vital interest to ourselves. This strategy of extended deterrence in turn has necessitated our move to counterforce targeting, which is bound up with our retention of the option of first use of nuclear weapons.

A brief review of counterforce might be in order here, to demonstrate how closely our strategic nuclear orientation, with its concomitant costs and dangers, is tied to our orientation to the protection of allies. The essence of counterforce is the use of some fraction of our strategic nuclear force to attack the enemy's military installations, logistical complexes, and—to put most important matters last—nuclear forces, including missiles in silos. To do the latter, we must acquire "hard target kill capability."

The interesting question is why we have arrived at counterforce, which, after all, warps our doctrine of response toward the first use of nuclear weapons, prejudicing crisis stability and increasing the likelihood of escalation to nuclear war. This targeting strategy has been misrepresented by the nuclear doves as a perversity, at best a mindless technical drift—and now, lately, a principal responsibility of the Reagan administration. On the other hand, it has been misconceived by some nuclear hawks as a general imperative of the overall strategic nuclear balance. But America's move to counterforce is not crazy or accidental, or merely generic. It is our specific adherence to alliance commitments that skews our strategy toward counterforce weapons and targeting.

The most convincing motive for counterforce is "damage limitation"—that is, restricting the damage to our society in the event of an enemy nuclear attack. Part of that motive must be to strike Soviet missiles in silos, to degrade the force the enemy would have available to use, in some stage of a nuclear exchange, to attack our society. Further, we can deduce that such a damage-limiting attack, to have its intended effect, must be preemptive.[23] Indirectly damage-limiting, our counterforce attack (in conjunction with anti-ballistic missile defense) would erode the enemy's ability to attack our nuclear forces; in turn, our surviving nuclear forces would be more amply available to deter his eventual attack on our cities by holding hostage his cities and perhaps residual objects of military value. Directly damage-limiting, our counterforce attack would erode the enemy's ability to attack our cities in his earliest nuclear move (though such a move would be irrational).

The credibility of our extended deterrence over Europe requires the practical invulnerability of our own society to Soviet attack—that is, the limitation to "tolerable" levels of casualties and destruction. This is so because few people believe that we would risk a hundred million

---

[23]This is not to accuse anyone of plotting a preventive war—the definition of which is a war, ex nihilo, to destroy our adversary before he reaches the point, allegedly, of waging a war to destroy our own country. By contrast, a preemptive strike is contingent and occurs only in an already developing confrontation.

American lives to spread our protective mantle over Western Europe and other parts of the world.

Counterforce, then, makes sense as an attempt to fulfill the requisite conditions of extended deterrence—and, it is fair to say, only as such. Thus our willingness to protect our allies rises or falls with the prospective viability of counterforce, and, more generally, with our ability to protect our own society from nuclear attack. If there is any doubt—technical, economic, political—that we will achieve that invulnerability, then what becomes of the validity of our extensive nuclear commitments, especially to Western Europe?

In fact, European leaders and analysts share this skepticism about American support. Our rhetorical assurances are seriously contradicted by our actions. They are also negated by our basic situation and interests, which differ from those of our European allies. Quite understandably, from our own perspective, we always seem to be putting time and distance between the outbreak of war in Europe and the decision to use our strategic nuclear weapons. Virtually any change in our military doctrine or posture—up, down, or sideways—can be seen to have the effect, if not the purpose, of "decoupling" us from Europe.

Even the alleged propensity of the Reagan administration to "limited nuclear war" has its origin and foundation in this logic. It is not something that began suddenly when Ronald Reagan planted his foot firmly in his mouth and said: "I could see where you could have the exchange of tactical weapons against troops in the field without it bringing either one of the major powers to pushing the button."[24] The doubts had been sown long before that—in a series of American moves: the MLF, the multilateral nuclear sharing scheme of the late 1950s and early 1960s; the emphasis on "flexible response" of the Kennedy-McNamara administration; the "Schlesinger Doctrine" of 1974, that contemplated the direct and selective use of the American strategic nuclear force; and the perennial interest in "mini-nukes," including such variants as the "neutron bomb." Even the new long-range theater nuclear weapons the United States began to emplace in Europe at the end of 1983—the Pershing IIs and the ground-launched cruise missiles—are ambiguous: They may enhance coupling by perfecting the essential link of theater nuclear weapons, but they also invoke the specter of restricting even a nuclear war to European territory. So Reagan's dim perception happened to be correct: Nuclear decoupling is America's "real" strategy.

What, then, of the preparations for "protracted nuclear war," spec-

---

[24]Interview with out-of-town editors at the White House, October 16, 1981.

ified in the famous Defense Guidance issued by Secretary Weinberger to the military Services?[25] Here, even the proviso that American nuclear forces must "prevail and be able to force the Soviet Union to seek earliest termination of hostilities on terms favorable to the United States" has a familiar ring to anyone who has worked and planned in the Pentagon during the past 20 years. But it is particularly redolent of the years of Jimmy Carter and his Secretary of Defense Harold Brown, who advanced the concept of prolonged, multiphase nuclear war, with the disabling of Soviet leadership and the sinews of the Soviet state. Also in the development of counterforce weapons, such as the MX, Trident II, and intermediate-range cruise missiles, the Carter administration was the precursor of the Reagan administration. PD-59, the August 1980 presidential directive that codified a nuclear war-fighting stance, was, in a sense, the first strategic act of the *Reagan* administration.

[25]"Fiscal Year 1984–1988 Defense Guidance," leaked to and summarized by *The New York Times*, in an article by Richard Halloran, May 30, 1982.

A Dilemma and an Alternative

We see, then, that the national strategy of the Reagan administration is a variant on the traditional American national strategy. What is wrong with it is not what is peculiar about it, but what has been wrong with the American paradigm itself for the past 40 years—at first only latently or incipiently, but by now grossly and obviously. The framework of deterrence and alliance is increasingly unstable, because its foundations are being eroded by objective factors in the world and in the American domestic system. In the world, there is the changing shape of the international system—an increasing diffusion of power, frustrating American intervention and making the extension of our "nuclear umbrella" more risky. At home, there are revolts against taxes and conscription, and resistance to the enlarged governmental authority necessary to sustain an ambitious foreign policy. Thus, the task now is to transcend partisan rhetoric and meretricious critical ploys and to find a real and major alternative to the structure of deterrence and alliance that has become so burdensome and precarious.

More important, perhaps, than any concrete prescription is the train of reason that leads to it. It is important how you make the case. The debate we are now having is on the wrong ground. It should not be a beauty competition of "attractive" values, a parade of wish lists for America and the world, or a succession of unsupported recommendations, however constructive some might be.

If we put forward a case for nonintervention, it will not be a pure prescription of a state of affairs that is inherently and universally attractive. Prescription must be mingled with prediction. Nonintervention must be proposed as an adjustment to the world as it is shaping up and to the constraints of our polity, society, and economy. Our national orientation should not depend entirely on whether some object is worthy of our commitment. Worthy causes are not free. As in all things, there is a price to be paid; and that price has been growing higher. The multidimensional costs of intervention (the specific acts and the general

35

stance of perpetual preparedness) should, and will, be weighed against the consequences of not intervening and not preparing to intervene. Part of the prediction is that our country, taken as a decision-making system, will not pay these costs.

In a sense, the national debate on defense is a contest in the shifting of the burden of proof. It is not proper to place the burden uniquely on one brand of critics, the noninterventionists, to construct a comprehensive alternative program that will reconcile all the contradictions in America's external and internal situations, to everyone's satisfaction, without pain or loss. Indeed, it would be ironically inappropriate to fasten that burden on those whose main point is that tough choice is inescapable.

Let me recapitulate, then, how I conceive of my alternative: first, as an accounting, a costing out; second, as a choice, a presentation of the conditions and consequences of attaining this alternative stance; third—and only third—as a decision to make that choice, to accept that alternative, with its comparative costs and its particular consequences. The point is that each of these phases is conceptually separate. One can take or leave the third phase, the decision, and still understand and perhaps even accept the validity of the first two phases.

As we have seen, the range of most contemporary critiques of foreign policy is not very wide. But, because the probable future state of the international system will be more intractable than most critics believe, and because our capacity to meet the conditions of *any* of their alternative interventionist strategies is much more inhibited than most critics understand, an "ideal" resolution of our dilemma would occasion a more wholesale remedy.

An appropriate remedy would require a large-scale cut in defense spending, on the order of $120 to $150 billion a year from current levels. (Another large amount, to close the budgetary gap that looms each year for the rest of this decade at least, would have to come from further stringent cuts in welfare entitlements and domestic government programs.) But if we are to cut defense spending significantly, we must change our national strategies and our foreign policy. For the only way to save significant sums from the defense budget is to remove large, noticeable units from the force structure. And this would make it necessary, somewhere along the line, to reduce our defensive commitments in the world.

Specifically, both of the cardinal elements of the present American strategic paradigm would have to change. Instead of deterrence and alliance, we would pursue war-avoidance and self-reliance. Our security would depend more on our abstention from regional conflicts and, in the strategic nuclear dimension, on what I would call "finite essential deterrence."

Self-reliance is a response to the dissolution of alliances, nuclear proliferation, and the practical demise of extended deterrence. Our military program would be designed to defend the most restricted perimeter required to protect our core values. Those core values are our political integrity and the safety of our citizens and their domestic property. That is a much smaller perimeter than the one we are now committed to defend. This does not imply a penitent retraction from a prior stance of gratuitous imperialism. To be critical of American intervention, it is not necessary to consider that the United States, in this phase of its history, has been expansionist or aggressive. Rather, I take it as axiomatic that we are reactive and essentially defensive in our national strategy, though not always in our tactics. We have been devoted fundamentally to our own safety and well-being and to our own valued political and social principles, though some false extensions of those objectives have drawn us into a series of destructive conflicts. Precisely because America's stance in the world is defensive, we would benefit from a compartmentalization of deadly quarrels between other nations. Linking these quarrels with regions contiguous to ourselves or with other issues directly impinging on ourselves are the ways in which local disturbances could be transformed into vital threats. Compartmentalization must mean delegating defensive tasks to regional countries, and accepting the results, win or lose. Over time, we would accommodate the dissolution of defensive commitments, including NATO, that obligate us contingently to overseas intervention.

(What would be the probable status of Europe without American protection? I would envisage a Europe that is independent politically and diplomatically, and autonomous strategically; that acts in greater military concert, though not political unity or strategic unanimity. Actually, Europe could go quite far toward defending itself without American help. It need not be "Finlandized," either in whole or in part. If the United States were to withdraw, the principal European countries would probably increase their defense spending gradually, perhaps to five or six percent of their gross national product. This would produce more absolute military output than the Soviet Union. Though the national defense budgets might be uncoordinated, this aggregate measure is not meaningless. No one can predict whether

Europe would opt to do this, but that would be Europe's choice, not ours.)[26]

This is not necessarily a prescription for instantly dismantling our formal alliances. In this century, old alliances seldom die; they waste away. They become drained of their real strategic content, and nations hedge against the guarantees that the alliances still pretend to offer. Something like that seems already to be happening to NATO, under the surface of the formalities, and under the cover of the energetic programs for modernizing and enhancing forces.

The concomitant is that we would encourage other nations to hedge, to become self-reliant. In fact, other countries that are foresighted already discount American protection in a wide range of possible cases, despite our formal obligations to come to their assistance. This does not imply that all these countries face imminent threats; simply that some are impressed more by American defaults than by American reassurances and have drawn the appropriate conclusions.

As for the United States, in this proposal we would defend against military threats directed against our homeland. That is not, in the first instance, an overtly geographical criterion, and deliberately not. We should not be fixated on drawing lines in the sand, though this is the simplest and most comprehensible exercise. Rather, we should be concerned to characterize correctly the nature and import of other countries' actions, and appreciate the characteristics of foreign events that cause us to consider them "threats." Functional criteria may be less definitive than geographical, but they are more important. In a program of nonintervention, the United States would defend against an umbra of direct threats to those values that are so basic that they are part of the definition of state and society: the autonomy of its political processes and the safety of U.S. citizens and their domestic property. Because those values are inalienable, their defense must be credible. We would also

---

[26]I have written in more detail about the strategic prospects of Europe without American protection, in *NATO's Unremarked Demise* (Berkeley, California: University of California, Institute of International Studies, 1979). Among other things, West Germany is a natural tank-trap, with wall-to-wall urbanization, belts of dense forest, and several "ditches" such as the Elbe, Saale, and Oder Rivers, to stop or delay first- and, if necessary, second-echelon Warsaw Pact forces. And the same conventional technology and reserve mobilization schemes that some strategists, such as Steven Canby, demonstrate would make the defensive task for the whole present alliance, including the United States, more feasible, would also demonstrably make the defensive task of the residual alliance, *without* the United States, at least feasible. (See, among many of his treatments of this issue, Steven Canby and Ingemar Dörfer, "More Troops, Fewer Missiles," *Foreign Policy*, Winter 1983–84.)

defend against a penumbra of challenges that are indirectly threatening but are relevant because of their weight, momentum, direction, and ineluctability. We would be looking for a new set of criteria—decision-rules, if you will—that condition and bound our responses to future events that could be considered challenges. This is an intensive, rather than extensive, definition.

The other phase of our counter-paradigm, war-avoidance, is a response to the diffusion of power, the attainment of nuclear parity by the Soviet Union, and the risk of nuclear destruction to ourselves. It is based on the fact that we can no longer intricately and reliably manipulate or "manage" conflict.

War-avoidance thus invokes primarily—though not exclusively—the strategic nuclear component of our counter-paradigm. We will always need a strategy that discourages direct nuclear attacks on our homeland, or intolerable coercion of our international political choices by nuclear threats. But today, given the parity between the nuclear arsenals of the two superpowers, our safety depends on maintaining a condition that is called "crisis stability," wherein both sides have a strong incentive to avoid striking first with their nuclear weapons.

A design for nuclear stability would go like this: Since an enemy's first strike must logically be a damage-limiting attack against our nuclear forces, we should eliminate our land-based systems as they become even theoretically vulnerable to a Soviet preemptive strike. These systems are inevitably vulnerable, despite the efforts of a succession of administrations to put them in multiple or closely-spaced shelters (as with the MX), or to acquire a redundant and dispersed force (as with the prospective "Midgetman" individual-warhead missiles). Instead, we should move to a diad of strategic nuclear forces: submarines, and bombers armed with medium-range air-launched cruise missiles. Then, in our targeting doctrine, to discourage further a Soviet first strike, we should not aim at Soviet missiles. (Nor does it make any strategic or moral sense to aim at Soviet cities.) Rather, we should develop a list of some 3,000 military targets, such as naval and air bases, concentrations of conventional forces, military logistical complexes, and arms industries that are relatively far from large civilian population centers.

Finally, since nuclear war is most likely to occur through *our* escalation in the midst of conventional war—probably in Europe, or possibly in the Middle East—we must confront our attitude toward the first use of nuclear weapons. I believe we should impose upon ourselves an unconditional doctrine of no first use of nuclear weapons. But several of the most prominent recent proposals for no first use do not satisfy the requisites of firm argumentation. An example is the article of McGeorge Bundy, George Kennan, Robert McNamara, and Gerard Smith, "Nuclear Weapons and the Atlantic Alliance."[27] These authors raise, but do not dispose of, questions that go beyond tactical doctrine to the heart of extended deterrence. They correctly respond to their primary fear, of the uncontrolled spread of nuclear war if we were to initiate it in Europe. But they complicate and ultimately defeat their own proposal by insisting on the integrity of the American defense of Western Europe against Soviet attack.

Unfortunately, the very fear of inevitable escalation of a local European conventional war to a global nuclear conflagration constitutes the essential element in the coupling of America's strategic nuclear arsenal to the local defense of its allies. The authors would reinforce the "firebreak" between conventional war and any use of nuclear weapons. But firebreaks are the antithesis of coupling. For extended deterrence to work, the escalatory chain, from conventional war to theater nuclear weapons to the use of America's ultimate strategic weapon, must seem to be unbroken.

The only way to square this circle would be to guarantee the conventional defense of Western Europe; and indeed the authors make their apparent renunciation of first use of nuclear weapons conditional on our acquisition of such a conventional defense. This is a currently fashionable argument; but those who reflexively opt for conventional defense cannot mean just any conventional effort. They must mean the high-confidence defense of Europe with conventional arms. And they have the further burden of not just exhorting the United States and its allies to do more to guarantee the integrity of Western Europe, but predicting that this is going to happen. To determine the feasibility—and thus the probability—of the conventional defense option, we must have a bill of costs. But nowhere do these authors, or other proponents of self-sufficient conventional defense, present that bill. Our share of the conventional defense of Europe—and this is not even designed to be a pure, high-confidence defense—is now $129 billion for 1985—more than 40 percent of the $305 billion requested by the Reagan administration for defense in 1985. Even these funds will hardly be forthcoming.

Thus, a consistent proposal of no first use of nuclear weapons implies the dissolution of our defensive commitment to NATO. Indeed, those who propose no first use of nuclear weapons without insuring our

[27]*Foreign Affairs*, Spring 1982.

successful conventional defense are implicitly advocating that the United States disengage from NATO. Their proposals simply gloss over, or fail to appreciate, the contradiction between crisis stability and deterrent stability. There is an essential tension, not an easy complementarity, between achieving safety for ourselves through crisis stability and achieving safety for the objects of our protection in the world through deterrent stability. The way—and the only way—we can lessen the incidence of this tension is by diminishing our obligations to extend defensive protection in any form. Crisis stability more closely coincides with deterrent stability as we shed external commitments and concentrate on our own defense.

The two elements of war-avoidance and self-reliance constitute a new paradigm. They amount to a principled policy of nonintervention that is consistent enough to merit the status of a major alternative. We would no longer consider peace to be seamless and indivisible. There might well be continuing troubles in the world, including cases where a Soviet-sponsored faction perpetrates a forcible revision of the local military balance. If we were to intervene, we might win a few rounds (witness the obvious example of Grenada in November 1983). But the list of feasible interventions is far shorter than the list of desirable ones, and is even shorter than the list of "necessary" ones.

In this new paradigm, interactions with other nations, groups, and interests in the world would continue; indeed, they would probably intensify and multiply. But we would no longer try to "manage" interdependence. Instead, we would hedge against conditions we could not control, and protect our security by reducing vulnerabilities to the practical minimum. We would emphasize our own fiscal soundness, private capital accumulation, and productivity. We would encourage substitutes for critical raw materials and energy, letting price structures reflect and ration scarcity and anticipate and mitigate risks.

Nonintervention has been carelessly and gratuitously labeled "isolationism." This ascription is an irrelevance and an anachronism. Yet it need not be abjectly denied. There may be a use for a more compartmentalized world—a world of buffers, insulation, and hedges, the discrimination of functions, the quarantining of other people's conflicts, even the acceptance of others' economic blocs if we cannot get something better, such as universal free trade, which is theoretically preferable but practically unlikely. In short, we would opt for the reality of adjustment rather than the illusion of control.

The design implied in this counter-paradigm is the compartmentalization of the international system in two senses, functional and geographical: the separation of political-military functions from social and economic functions; and the strategic separation of regions. This is obviously the opposite of the "interdependence" about which we are constantly lectured, breathlessly or sententiously. More interdependence is prescribed as a homeopathic cure for the ills of interdependence. But, when stripped of its happy verbal aura, it represents the overdependence of each nation upon others. It is not a condition that any nation would suffer if it could avoid it.

Others may be tempted to measure such an anarchical world, with its liabilities, against the abstract desirability of controlling events, steering them in favorable directions. But—somewhat like deterrence—attempts at control, if they fail, can yield both greater implication and greater harm for the nation that has made the attempt. Whereas, if we avoid involvement, there may be disorder in the world, but we are compensated by the fact that we are not implicated in it.

A Counter-Budget

If we were to consider a fundamentally different national strategy and foreign policy, the proposition would go in two directions: (1) We can make large cuts in the defense budget—not marginal changes, but a fiscal harvest on the order of 45 percent of our entire defense budget—*if* we severely limit our foreign policy objectives. But (2) large cuts in the defense budget can be made *only if* there is a fundamental change in American foreign policy.

Thus, a counter-budget based on noninterventionist assumptions about American foreign policy is not elusive or arcane. It does not require detailed expertise in weapons characteristics or intimate knowledge of quirks of procurement. It is not particularly sensitive to minute inside information on defense costing. When we are talking about $5 trillion that the United States may spend over a decade, large aggregates will do very nicely to illustrate the differences an alternative policy could make.

I will specify the force structure and the budgetary costs derived from a noninterventionist foreign policy and national strategy. It is not my intent to attract disproportionate critical attention to these numbers. My intent is to break with the negligent tradition of critics who promise great improvements and savings but do not attach price tags. It is hard to know what critics are trying to say if they don't reveal the forces and the defense budgets that go along with their proposals. The elements of the alternative policy and strategy that I propose—war-avoidance and self-reliance—are not mere rhetorical counters. They make real differences in forces and deployments, weapons and doctrines, defense budgets and manpower requirements.

In this alternative proposal, we would design our general purpose forces to be "second chance" forces. If the worst happened, and all calculations were proved wrong (this would be nothing less than a momentous, cumulative, relentless military threat directed against our own country), we would want to have maintained a core of defensive units and activities to hold vital positions and form the basis on which to rebuild our strength. We would always have kept strategic nuclear forces capable of deterring direct nuclear attacks on our own homeland. But those requirements are much less demanding than the multifarious capabilities required by extended deterrence, the attempt to spread our nuclear mantle over other nations and other interests.

We could defend our essential security and our central values with a much smaller force structure than we now have—let alone what the Reagan administration might create if it were able to obtain the resources. Such a force structure would provide the following general purpose forces: 8 land divisions (6 Army and 2 Marine), 20 tactical air wing equivalents (11 for the Air Force, 4 for the Marines, and 5 for the Navy), and 6 carrier battle groups. With the addition of two-pronged nuclear forces of submarines and cruise-missile-armed bombers, this would mean manpower of 1,185,000 men (Army 370,000, Air Force 315,000, Navy 365,000, Marine Corps 135,000). The total defense budget at the end of a decade of adjustment would be about $154 billion in 1985 dollars. In contrast, the Reagan administration has requested, for 1985, 20 land divisions and 44 tactical air wing equivalents, with 13 carrier battle groups; this force requires 2,166,000 men and $305 billion.

One doesn't need a micrometer to measure those differences, and they will multiply enormously unless we change our course. The way we're headed, the defense budget will be close to $700 billion by 1994, and cumulative defense spending during that decade will be $4.8 trillion. Under a noninterventionist policy, the 1994 defense budget would be 45 percent less and the cumulative cost over a decade would be $2.6 trillion.

If the United States were to decide to adopt such a sharply lower defense budget, how might we get from here to there? Given the consideration that we would not want to, and would not be able to, shift and demobilize forces overnight (indeed, the process of disengagement and reduction that I propose should take from five to ten years, depending on the region affected), I would make a modest "zero-growth" proposal: Take the defense budget originally requested by the Reagan administration for Fiscal Year 1984 ($258 billion), add 5 percent for inflation (this comes to $271 billion), and use this figure as a starting point for our proposed FY 1985 budget. Then hold this steady for a decade, in current ("then-year") dollars, despite inflation (at the rate assumed in the Reagan administration's 1985 defense budget for the first five years and 5 percent thereafter) and with no real cost growth. The resulting schedule of proposed defense expenditures for the ten-year period would approximate my proposal of gradual reductions to $154 billion a year in 1985 dollars but allowing countervailingly for inflation. It would amount to a "freeze" in defense spending at President Reagan's own request for 1984.

Conclusion: The Verdict of History

The task for American foreign policy and national strategy is not simple and direct, as many would have it; it is complex and highly conditional. It is not simply to oppose Soviet military threats in the way that has become traditional since the beginning of the Cold War; or even, more broadly, to obstruct organized collectivist or revolutionary forces in the world. It is to do this only in cases that are truly necessary to the interests of our citizens and constituent groups of our society, and in a way that will not prejudice the values that underpin our own system. In other words, we must find a foreign policy and a national strategy that are appropriate to our economy, our liberties, and the character of American society. That is a much more formidable challenge.

The beginning of wisdom is to become clear about our situation. This kind of analysis does not tell us what to do. But it should sharpen our sense of the available alternatives. The choice is not among ideal programs and states of affairs, unencumbered by their entailed requirements and effects. Without confronting those hard conditions and results, we would be opting for illusions. What makes solutions probable is not their attractiveness or political acceptability. What makes them likely, even historically inevitable, is that the other attempted courses will fail.

In this sense, the proposed "middle" courses of other critics—military reform, selective intervention, and the rest—when their contradictions are analyzed and their shortcomings are understood, only lead us back to our more fundamental options: On the one hand, there is the program of high defense budgets, comprehensive and sustained preparations, vast forces, far-ranging deployments, and heightened threats of military response backed by prompt and extensive movements close to the brink of encounter—in short, what we have now. On the other hand, there is the course of disengagement, which might become more plausible in the light of the comparison.

ABOUT THE AUTHOR

Earl C. Ravenal, a former official in the Office of the Secretary of Defense, is a professor of international relations at the Georgetown University School of Foreign Service. He is an adjunct scholar and a member of the Board of Directors of the Cato Institute. Prof. Ravenal is the author of *Never Again: Learning from America's Foreign Policy Failures, NATO's Unremarked Demise, Strategic Disengagement and World Peace*, and numerous other books and articles on American foreign and military policy. He received his B.A. from Harvard University and his M.A. and Ph.D. from The Johns Hopkins University School of Advanced International Studies.

Date Due

Cato Institute

Founded in 1977, the Cato Institute is a public policy research foundation dedicated to broadening the parameters of policy debate to allow consideration of more options that are consistent with the traditional American principles of limited government, individual liberty, and peace. Toward that goal, the Institute strives to achieve a greater involvement of the intelligent, concerned lay public in questions of policy and the proper role of government.

The Institute is named for *Cato's Letters,* pamphlets that were widely read in the American Colonies in the early eighteenth century and played a major role in laying the philosophical foundation for the revolution that followed. Since that revolution, civil and economic liberties have been eroded as the number and complexity of social problems have grown. Today virtually no aspect of human life is free from the domination of a governing class of politico-economic interests. A pervasive intolerance for individual rights is shown by government's arbitrary intrusions into private economic transactions and its disregard for civil liberties.

To counter this trend the Cato Institute undertakes an extensive publications program dealing with the complete spectrum of policy issues. Books, monographs, and shorter studies are commissioned to examine the federal budget, social security, regulation, NATO, international trade, and a myriad of other issues. Major policy conferences are held throughout the year from which papers are published thrice-yearly in the *Cato Journal.* The Institute maintains an informal joint publishing arrangement with the Johns Hopkins University Press.

In order to maintain an independent posture, the Cato Institute accepts no government funding. Contributions are received from foundations, corporations, and individuals, and other revenue is generated from the sale of publications. The Institute is a non-profit, tax-exempt, educational foundation under Section 501(c)3 of the Internal Revenue Code.

CATO INSTITUTE
224 Second St., S.E.
Washington, D.C. 20003